BAPTISTS
AND
LOCAL AUTONOMY

BAPTISTS AND LOCAL AUTONOMY

*The Development, Distortions, Decline
And New Directions of Local Autonomy
in Baptist Churches*

Howard R. Stewart

Foreword by
HARVEY A. EVERETT
*Associate General Secretary for Field Operations
American Baptist Churches in the U.S.A.*

EXPOSITION PRESS HICKSVILLE, NEW YORK

Dedicated to
MR. W. G. "BILL" DAVIS
of Dover, Delaware
Faithful to Christ
A loyal friend

FIRST EDITION

ISBN 0-682-48030-4

Printed in the United States of America

Contents

Foreword

The author has found insights regarding Baptists and their structural expression of the faith, that heretofore have not been encompassed in a single volume. Autonomy becomes, in this author's work, a positive expression. However, he does not minimize the problems that this form of churchly expression has, can and does bring, but he breaks through with insights how those negative dimensions can, and have been, and are being changed in various ways.

The Biblical undergirding of this book is especially helpful, as Baptists being "people of the Book" need to know the rootage of their life. The author does this beautifully and with such style that the sentences flow in such a way as to carry the reader through the book in an attitude of expectancy and excitement.

A careful reading of the first two chapters is most rewarding, as the author has in a few pages shared the major changes in emphasis, and how they came about, which makes clear many of the aspects of Baptist life today and how they evolved.

"The Changing Scene in the Twentieth Century" chapter helps the reader to see the struggle the Baptists have had between two dominant characteristics—the desire for efficiency and the protection of autonomy of the local congregations, and units they form for mission expression. This insight, the resulting studies, attempts and partial successes at reorganization to achieve both to the maximum degree, make fascinating reading for any individual interested in knowing how we came to be the way we are and the events and forces which made it a reality.

The final chapter, "Recovery in These Latter Days," is one of the best expressions of Baptist directions today and the struggles to achieve it. In a few pages the author gets to the heart of the movement, and indicates both the blessings and problems that the dealing with the issue of autonomy has brought for Baptists, regardless of denominational group-

ing. It is a must chapter for any person just becoming a
Baptist, and periodically required reading for any pastor to
regain the perspective on who we are and how we came to
be this way. Such careful and periodic study will help us
avoid in the future, the mistakes and events of history and
will assist us in building on the efforts of those who fought
these battles before us.

Baptists and Local Autonomy is long overdue. In a single
volume the author has let us see this cardinal principle
which has been both a blessing and a curse as it has affected
the life and mission of Baptists through the years.

The author sees real hope for Baptists as he states in his
concluding chapter: "Now near the three-quarter mark of
the twentieth century they [Baptists] stand at the brink of
Jordan ready to cross over into Canaan. The older generation died in the wilderness, and a new generation of Baptists
seem about to possess the land. . . If Baptists succeed in
entering the promised land of a visible form of the church
which is both Biblical and Baptist they will enjoy the milk
and honey of an era of witness, worship and fellowship
beyond anything they have ever known." The beautiful
thing about these words is they are more than words. They
are a verbalization of what is happening. Howard Stewart in
his new book has brought hope, direction and a clarification
for Baptists in dealing with their biggest stumbling block
and yet potentially one of their biggest blessings properly
used—autonomy, and a Baptist understanding of the church
as the body of Christ.

HARVEY A. EVERETT
Associate General Secretary
for Field Operations
American Baptist Churches in the U.S.A.

One

Our Beginnings in Congregationalism

To understand Baptist principles one must go back to the English Reformation. Out of that movement, particularly the Puritan and Congregational forms of it, the Baptists emerged. Therefore, an understanding of Baptist polity and practice requires a comprehension of the Congregationalist concept of the church.

In its beginnings in the sixteenth century, Puritanism was directed toward a reform of the Church of England from within. A period of exile in Geneva had provided the English Reformers with a demonstration of John Calvin's religious politics founded upon the Word of God. With the accession of Elizabeth to the throne in 1558, they looked for the triumph of Protestantism and the imposition of Calvinism upon England. Their hopes were never realized, however, as Elizabeth did little or nothing to eliminate the evils in the church. She resisted all efforts to reform the church from within or without. There were those who demanded immediate reform, but the firm policies of the Queen held them in check. Though their activities were restricted, the Puritans utilized this period to develop their concepts of the church.

In the minds of many of the Puritans the Scriptures taught presbyterianism rather than episcopacy as the proper form of church government. Along with the Anglicans, Lutherans, Zwinglians, and Calvinists they believed the State's highest function to be the external welfare of the church and the support of its censures. Obedience to civil law was enjoined on all except when the law transgressed the commands of God. For the unity of the church and nation the Puritans believed the church should remain

9

national in structure, with everyone required to be a member.

However, belief in a church which comprised an entire nation seemed in conflict with the doctrine of predestination. If certain people were destined to perdition, how could they be counted as members of the church? The Puritans and Anglicans resolved the conflict by pronouncing the nonelect as "in" the church, but not "of" the church. They might "have fellowship in the outward things, but they can have no part in effectual and saving grace."[1] This solution to the problem, however, was unacceptable to a new breed of Puritans beginning in 1581 with Robert Browne of Norfolk.

Although he later recanted, Robert Browne was the forerunner of these new Puritans who advocated separation from the established church. At Cambridge he had been exposed to the preaching of Thomas Cartwright, the "Cambridge Reformer," but he went beyond his teacher's ideas. In his view, membership should be restricted to persons who gave suitable evidence of belonging to the elect. Such congregations were called "gathered churches" in contrast to the more comprehensive "parish churches." After several years of persecution, imprisonments, and exile Browne renounced his program of separation, returned to England, and took a country church. His ideas, however, gained a following and led to the Congregationalist movement. After his defection, his followers disavowed his leadership, but they espoused the cause of Congregationalism. While they advocated Congregational principles they differed in their opinions on separation from the established church, so they were divided into separating and nonseparating congregations. Numbered among the leaders were such men as William Ames, Francis Johnson, John Robinson, and most important for Baptists, John Smyth.

John Smyth was a man who made a rapid series of steps from Anglicanism to Puritanism, to Congregationalism, to Separatism, and ultimately Baptist. He had been tutored by

Francis Johnson at Cambridge where he became a fellow in 1594, served as lecturer at Lincoln from 1600 to 1602, and in 1606 turned up as pastor of a group of Congregationalists at Gainesborough.[2] Because they were committed to a course of separation, the group was forced into exile in Holland in 1608. It was out of Smyth's congregation that the first Baptist church developed. Hence it is important to understand some of the principles by which the Congregationalists were governed in their thinking about the church.

An understanding of Congregationalism begins with its concept of the church. The church polity of the Congregationalists had two features which distinguished it from the Presbyterianism of the Puritans. In the first place, the Calvinism of the Puritans brought everyone into the visible church, but pronounced the elect as the true church. The Congregationalists, however, affirmed that only the elect should be in the visible church. These elect persons were to be gathered together to form true churches with Christ as their head. Christian character and confession of faith were to be the criteria used to judge a person's status as one of the elect. Such a church was distinguished not by the ministry of the Word and the administration of the sacraments, but by the "faith" and "order" of the gathered believers. These believers were bound by covenant in obedience to Jesus Christ and the civil laws. A willingness to adhere to the covenant was considered evidence that such a person had "been received into the covenant of grace with God himself."[3] The local, visible church thus became a colony of heaven on earth, an expression of the invisible church.

Secondly, the Congregationalists advocated local autonomy rather than the superstructure of the Presbyterians or Anglicans. Because each believer was one of God's elect, he had direct access to God. Each group of such persons was a self-sufficient entity and "competent to manage its own affairs" free from any external pressure. Representative assemblies such as Synods and Councils might advise the churches, but could exercise no authority over them. The kingdom on earth would thus be composed of many little groups of people who had given evidence of their election and were directing the affairs of the local assemblies according to the will of Christ. The Congregationalists were convinced that since all members were God's chosen people they would be of one mind in their decisions.

Congregationalists thus believed that primitive Christian churches were not "Diocesan Churches, but Particular Ordinary Congregations and the Bishops, as they were particularly called after the Apostles, were only parishional, not Diocesan Bishops, differing from Pastors only in priority of order, not majority of rule."[4] While each congregation was independent and not subject to ecclesiastical authority, together they constituted the universal church. Despite the emphasis on local autonomy they recognized the need for corporate association. As a contemporary said:

> Yet particular churches, as their Communion doth require, the light of nature and equity of rules and examples of Scripture doe teach, may and oftentimes also ought to enter into mutuall confederacy and fellowship among themselves in Classes and Synods, that they may use their common consent and mutuall helpe as much as fitly may be, in those things especially which are of greater moment; but the combination doth neither constitute a new forme of a church, neither ought to take away or diminish any way, that liberty and power which Christ hath left to his churches, for the directing and furthering whereof it only serves.[5]

The Church for the Congregationalists then was composed only of believers in Christ, the elect of God who were gathered together in particular churches and governed themselves free from external ecclesiastical authority. The outstanding feature by which the believers distinguished themselves as the elect was the taking of a church covenant upon the public confession of faith. The covenant was the instrument by which the church could identify him as such.

Herein lies the heart of Congregationalism—the free association of people by a covenant. Hence no coercion could compel an individual to join a church or force a church to receive an individual. A church composed of such people bound by a covenant would be an indication of their membership in the covenant of God's grace. Whatever may be involved in the organization by way of ministry, administration, or discipline was to be created by the body after taking the covenant. Such an arrangement was the government of the church subject to the mind of the society as they interpreted the Scriptures. The covenant then gave "constitution and being to the visible church."[6] How far did this church power extend?

Since the organization was the creation of the people, they were the ones to decide whether or not any facet of their church life was in agreement with their covenant. For example, officers, leaders, and ministers were selected by the people and were responsible to them. Furthermore, the authority of those elected to office was contingent upon the voluntary subjection of the people to their rule. If a person was to be excommunicated, the whole church must be convinced that the cause for the excommunication was justified. The whole church, however, was bound by the rule of the Bible. This church power or authority found its expression in the church meeting.

The church meeting was a regular meeting of all members of particular church in good standing for the purpose of taking counsel together and reaching decisions on all matters related to the life of the church. Daniel Jenkins has suggested some important aspects of the church meeting.[7] It provided the congregation with a concrete opportunity to seek the will of God in specific matters. Secondly, it was also an opportunity for the members to exercise responsible discipline in seeking God's will rather than the unbridled speaking of one's mind. Thirdly, it required on the part of the members a deliberate effort to seek the mind of Christ rather than the desires of individuals or groups. In the fourth place, it required of the congregation a recognition that some matters are better handled by a delegated group. This would be especially true in matters related to censure, discipline, and excommunication.

The fact is laws governing discipline in the Congregational church were specifically outlined and administered by the elders who were impowered by the congregation. It was the duty of the minister and the elders to question any accused person and to prepare the case against him if warranted. The people were then presented with the case for a ruling. Thus in discipline, as in all phases of their church life, the Congregationalists insisted on the right of the local church to be governed by Christ.

The Congregationalists believed this freedom enabled the church more adequately to be the voice of Christ, without interference by the state or any other power. If Christians, the rulers themselves were subject to the same polity and discipline as the rest of the church. They defined the limits of freedom in terms of their concept of the church. Since they had the correct understanding of the Scriptures, if followed that they were the true church. To tolerate other sects was out of the question. The Congregationalists believed it was the duty of the state to suppress and root out all false religions; that is, non-Congregationalist religions. Such a certainty of conviction of their position was imbedded in their regard for the Scriptures as taught by their ministers.

According to Congregational doctrine the call to the ministry could only be issued by Christ, but the church would become the means by which the call became a reality. It was Christ who gave gifts and abilities, but the church made possible the exercise of those gifts and abilities. However, the selection and call of the ministers was the responsibility of the congregation. Furthermore, the minister's authority was limited to his own parish, and then only as the congregation agreed to submit themselves to his authority. The minister was to order his calling according to the rule of Scripture.

The Bible was "not partial, but perfect rule of faith and manners" for Congregational life. The worship, ordinances, discipline, and doctrines were completely defined in the Scriptures. The Congregationalists further believed all necessary truth was clearly self-evident in Scripture without assistance from any other source.

These principles of the Congregationalists were based on their concept of the church, and were carried over into Baptist beginnings through John Smyth's congregation at Amsterdam. It was in the seed bed of the English Reformation that the grains of Puritan and Congregational concepts were nurtured and ultimately came to flower in the Baptists of seventeenth-century England.

Two

Baptists and Congregationalism

Baptist beginnings in seventeenth-century English Congregationalism can be traced to a Congregational Church organized at Gainesborough-on-Trent in 1602. By 1606, the church, for the sake of convenience, divided into two groups. One group met at Scrooby Manor House under the leadership of Richard Clifton while the other remained at Gainesborough with John Smyth as the pastor. Persecution soon drove the the Gainesborough group to Holland in 1608, where they settled at Amsterdam on property owned by a Mennonite merchant. Smyth was soon joined by Thomas Helwys in the leadership of the church. The Scrooby Manor congregation, now under the leadership of John Robinson, arrived at the same destination, only to move to Leyden, from where they sailed for the New World in 1620.

In the meantime, by 1609, under the influence of the Mennonites, Smyth accepted the concept of believer's baptism. He then proceeded to baptize himself, Helwys, and many of his congregation by affusion. The continuing Mennonite influence soon led Smyth and some of his members to petition for acceptance into the Mennonite fold. This action caused Helwys and ten others to part company with the Smyth faction. Smyth himself died in August of 1612, and the remainder of his followers joined the Mennonites on January 20, 1615.[1] With his small band Helwys returned to London and began holding meetings at Spitalfield outside the city walls. This General Baptist Church is the first Baptist Church on English soil for which there is historic proof.[2] The name General Baptist Church was applied because of belief in a general atonement as over against the Particular Baptist concept of a limited atonement.

The genesis of Particular Baptist Churches in England can be traced to a congregation lead by John Spilsbury in 1538. The church had its inception as a Separatist congregation organized at Southwark, London in 1616 under the leadership of Henry Jacob, who led the church for six years until he moved to Virginia in 1622. John Lathrop became pastor in 1625, and after two years in prison (1633-1634) took thirty members to New England to escape further persecution. In 1633, while Lathrop was in prison, a group of members separated from the church over a question on the administration of baptism and formed a new congregation. In 1638 they were joined by another group who also accepted believer's baptism. This group, with John Spilsbury as their pastor, became the first Particular Baptist Church in England. The Particular Baptists, as well as the General Baptists, shared many common theological concepts with the Congregationalists.

Particular Baptists and Congregationalists stayed very close to the typical Calvinism of the time. General Baptists differed only in their understanding of the atonement and the importance of the human will in salvation. It was their conception of the church which set both Baptists and Congregationalists apart from the other reformers.

Both Baptists and Congregationalists believed that the church was composed of individuals in a given geographical area who have been gathered by Christ through a common faith in Him. They also believed the local church to be vested with complete church power predicated upon the Word of God, and thus both groups were congregational in polity and practice. However, Baptists differed from Congregationalists on the manner by which the church expressed itself in visible form to the world.

While Baptists shared with Congregationalists the concept of a church membership composed only of regenerate persons, the Baptists insisted that believer's baptism should be the means of insuring this regenerate membership. To the Congregationalists the baptism of their children was the sign of the covenant relationship until the experience of conversion took place. Baptists, on the other hand, believed that baptism was evidence that a work of grace had already taken place and which was therefore only for believers.

Secondly, Congregationalists of seventeenth-century England believed it to be the duty of the state to enforce and protect the true faith; viz., Congregationalism. Baptists rejected this concept on two grounds. First, because the Kingdom of God was spiritual it could not be imposed by temporal power. Secondly, because a gathered church required that the church members individually and as a group be free to obey Christ.

Thirdly, Congregationalism was content to limit the church to the local congregation. In Congregational belief Christianity consisted of "myriad little groups . . . all managing their own affairs in accordance with rules delivered by Christ."[3] On the other hand Baptists insisted that the church was not merely a local group of believers, but they also expressed belief in the universal church through their associational life.[4]

An understanding of the Baptist view of the church also

requires a recognition of the importance of confessions of
faith. These confessions were not polemic in purpose, but
were intended to define the Baptist position and to justify
the existence of Baptists as a distinct Christian group. Such
confessions "have ever been simply manifestos of prevailing
doctrine in particular groups."[5] The Baptist confessions are
also important because of their historic connections. The
English Separatists made some minor changes in the Westminster Confession of Faith and adopted it as the Savoy
Declaration in 1658. Having made a few changes the Particular Baptists also adopted the Westminster Confession as
their own declaration in 1677 and reaffirmed it in 1689. This
same London Confession was adopted by the Philadelphia
Association in 1742. The differences between it and the
original Westminster Confession and the Savoy Declaration
indicate the points at which Baptists saw themselves differing
from Presbyterians and Congregationalists. Baptist confessions in general contain certain basic emphasis on congregational polity, believer's baptism, and associational life.

The principle of congregationalism, as practiced by the
Baptists, means the local church should, under Christ, exercise its own authority and regulate its own affairs. This
authority they referred to as "church power." A church has
to have discipline, a properly appointed leadership, a faithful preaching of God's Word, and regular observance of the
sacraments.[6] Entrance into this community of believers was
by the experience of conversion and believer's baptism.

The most distinctive contribution of seventeenth-century
Baptists to the Christian concept of the church was believer's
baptism.[7] In the minds of the Baptists the church was not
built upon the covenant by which members agreed to walk
together in all the ways of God. Rather it was built upon
the baptism with water in the name of the Father, Son and
Holy Spirit. Thus was the church constituted upon God's
action in redemption rather than agreement men made with
God and with one another. Indeed, to these Baptists, the
church was a company of baptized believers and the practice

of infant baptism was wholly inconsistent with the concept of the gathered church.

English Baptists were Congregationalists, but not Independents; that is, they believed in a gathered church which was in a living way associated with the universal church. Upon this principle they shared each other's fellowship and consulted together in deliberative assembly. The Baptist view of the church considered the local congregation as a part of the whole church, howbeit a true and complete expression of it. Associations among the Baptists were not regarded as optional and secondary but a necessary expression of Christian fellowship and of the universal church. Associational life developed to such a degree that by 1660 the General Baptists formed a General Assembly or annual meeting of all their associations in England. Particular Baptists also organized a General Assembly in 1689, when they were granted religious freedom by the Toleration Act of that year. In the American Colonies the associational principle found its earliest and most significant expression in the Philadelphia Association formed in 1707.

Three

Baptist Associational Life in America

The faith and life of Baptists in America was predominantly that of seventeenth-century English Particular Baptists. Thus, on July 27, 1707, five Particular Baptist churches in the middle colonies formed the Philadelphia Baptist Association along the lines of their sister associations in Britain. In contrast to the General Baptists who adopted a more centralized form of associational life, the Particular Baptist structure was loose and without power or authority over its member churches.

The importance of the Philadelphia Baptist Association cannot be overemphasized as it touched at least five major facets of Baptist life in America. In the first place, all major Baptist bodies in the United States stem from the Philadelphia Association.[1] Secondly, the Philadelphia Association served as something of a national organization for many years.[2] Thirdly, its pattern of organization was followed as many new associations were formed.[3] Fourthly, the Philadelphia Baptist Association provided a source of guidance and unity at a critical period in the development of Baptist life in America.[4] Finally, the Philadelphia Baptist Confession was the most influential of all Baptist confessions in the United States until it passed into the background of Baptist life in the nineteenth century.[5] Thus it may be seen that an examination of the Philadelphia Baptist Association will reveal the general pattern of all Baptists associational life in eighteenth-century America.

In their passion to preserve "local autonomy," present-day Baptists believe that traditional Baptist polity will not permit the delegating of authority on behalf of a local church. Hiscox states this position as follows:

> The delegates, or messengers, who compose the Council, are in no sense *representatives* of the church which appoint them. They cannot therefore act for their churches, to bind them by their action. *A Baptist Church cannot be represented* in any other body; nor can it transfer its authority or its function to any persons either within, or external to itself, to act for it. It can send messages by messengers, but it cannot delegate its power to act.[6]

However, such a position does not seem to be supported by early Baptist polity or practice. From their beginnings Baptists have encouraged their churches of like faith and order to manifest their oneness by forming Associations. The local churches elected delegates, representatives or messengers to act on their behalf at these Associations. Such a delegation of authority is evident in the terminology used in the Minutes of the Philadelphia Baptist Association. The Association required such authority if it were to fulfill its function and realize its purpose.[7]

The primary purpose of the Association as stated at the organization of the Philadelphia Association in 1707 was "to consult together about such things as are wanting in the churches" and take the necessary steps to "set them in order."[8] The churches were expected to accept the judgment of the Association. Such a concept mystifies latter-day Baptists, but our Baptist forbears were careful to define the limits of Associational power.

While the early Baptists clearly stated that the Association had no power over the local churches, they also made it quite clear that the Association was to deal with matters of concern within the local churches. A discipline entitled "A Short Treatise of Church Discipline," which was published by the Philadelphia Association in 1743, expressed the Association's concept of its power.

> For as much as it falls out many times that particular churches have to do with doubtful and difficult matters or differences in point of doctrine or administration . . . ; it is according to the mind of Christ that many churches holding communion together should meet by their messengers and delegates to consider of, and to give advice, in or about such matters in difference. . . . And such messengers and delegates, convened in the name of Christ by the voluntary consent of the several churches in such mutual communion, *may declare and determine* the mind of the Holy Spirit revealed in Scripture concerning things in difference, and *may decree the observation of things* that are true and necessary because revealed and appointed in Scripture. And *the churches will do well to receive, own, and observe such determinations,* on the evidence and authority of the mind of the Holy Ghost in them. . . . Yet *such delegates thus assembled are not entrusted or armed with any coercive power* or superior jurisdiction over the churches concerned, so as to impose

their determinations on them or their officers *under penalty of excommunication* or the like.[9]

Two factors in Baptist Associational life are evident in the above statement. On the one hand, the Association did not have the power to ordain, to censure or to excommunicate an individual. Such power belonged to the local church alone.[10] However, it assumed that the judgment of the Association represents the mind of Christ in a given matter, that the local church was expected to observe the determination of the Association.

On the other hand while the Association could not impose its advice, the local church was not free to reject such counsel of the Association and remain in fellowship with other churches of the Association. Such practice was based on the concept that the Association was not a collection of different churches. Instead, churches were admitted to the Association when it was determined that their faith and practice were in accord with the standards of the Associations. Furthermore, such a view permitted the Association to withdraw fellowship from any church that departed from its standards.

The Baptists recognized two important characteristics of the Association as they organized it. First, the Association was compared to a church of congregational polity. The delegates, though not possessing "church-power" over the churches or members, nonetheless constituted "one church." Thus they could "act in the name of Christ," order their corporate life, and as a congregation, discipline disorderly churches. Thus every church stood in the same relation to its association as a member to his church.[11]

Secondly, it made possible the maintenance of the delicate balance between the authority of the Association and the faithfulness of the churches, and thus the ability to steer a middle course between ecclesiastical tyranny and ecclesiastical irresponsibility. The Association was only as strong as the member churches made it by carrying out its determinations. Yet the Associations could only take away from the churches what it gave them; namely, the communion of all the churches.

The association was not an appendage of Baptist life, but a necessary expression of the Baptist concept of the church. The churches were to select their most capable members as representatives to the Association as well as provide for their expenses and business responsibilities at home.[12] The important task of seeking the mind of Christ in the life of the Association required the full representation of all the churches for which it spoke. The Philadelphia Association disciplined churches which failed to send a messenger or letter for three years by exclusion. Ministers were admonished to keep the Association meeting dates free of all appointments.[13] By thus stressing the importance of participation in its life, the Association was to "determine" and "declare" the mind of Christ." While it could not impose the "determination" upon a church, the church as a member of the Association was not free to reject it. The church was expected to own and receive the "determination" because it represented the ultimate authority of Christ. Such a concept was rooted in the belief that the Church was divine both in its original and continuing authority.

Throughout their history Baptists have maintained that the church consists of all who are under the Lordship of Christ and those persons are gathered together in local congregations. The church universal and the local congregations both operate under the Lordship of Christ as head of the church. Three articles of the Second London Confession of 1677, later the Philadelphia Confession, express this belief.

1. The Catholic or universal Church, which (with respect to internal work of the Spirit, and truth of grace) may be called invisible, consists of the whole number of the Elect, that have been, are, or shall be gathered into one under Christ the head thereof; and is the spouse, the Body, the fulness of him that filleth all in all.

2. All persons throughout the world professing the faith of the Gospel, and obedience unto God by Christ, according unto it; not destroying their own profession by any errors

everting the foundation; or unholiness of conversation are and may be called visible saints; and of such ought all particular congregations be constituted.

3. The Lord Jesus Christ is the Head of the Church, in whom by the appointment of the Father all power for the calling, institution, order, or Government of the Church, is invested in a supreme and sovereign manner. . . .[14]

Baptists, then, believe the origin of the church to be "in the incarnation, the Cross, the Resurrection and the descent of the Holy Spirit."[15] This divine origin gives the church certain unique characteristics including separation, purpose, and community.

The church is characterized by God's divine choice and its separation (I Peter 2:9-10). It was the activity of God in Jesus Christ which brought the church into being, and it is the response of faith to Christ which brings a person into the church (I Peter 2:4-8). Furthermore the church was given the divine purpose of declaring the wonderful deeds of Him who called them out of darkness into His marvelous light (I Peter 2:9-10). The response of faith brings a person into a unique community.

> After the descent of the Holy Spirit, the followers of Christ continued stedfastly in the apostles' teaching and (in the) fellowship (Koinōnio), in the breaking of bread and the prayers (Act 2:42 ASV). The use of the article with koinōnia distinguishes it from the apostles' teaching and indicates that the disciples were occupied constantly with four distinct activities of which the koinōnia, the fellowship, was one.[16]

Thus it may be seen that Baptists believed that both their local autonomy and associational life were not ends in themselves, but means to the end of determining the mind of Christ, the Lord of the church. Associational life functioned in several ways to realize this end.

One major function of the Association was the opportunity it afforded the churches to "upbuild one another in love." For several years prior to the organization of the Philadelphia Baptist Association the churches of Middletown, Piscataway, Cohansey, and Philadelphia had developed the custom of meeting together for baptism, the Lord's Supper, ordination, and inspirational preaching. To share the benefits of these meetings with those unable to attend, a circular letter was passed among the member churches to be read to the congregations. Along with words of encouragement, the letters usually contained same discussion of doctrine, Christian duty, or missionary endeavor. It was out of these general meetings that the Philadelphia Association was formed in 1707.[17]

A second area of concern in the Association was the provision of a duly qualified ministry for the churches. This task required the development of regulations and procedures for the recruitment, education, ordination, and placement of ministers. Because of the recurring problem of troublesome itinerant preachers it became necessary to set up strict regulations. The Philadelphia Association required that no man would be allowed to preach among the churches of the Association unless he produced credentials attesting his membership in his church and of his call and license to preach. All new ministers were required to be examined and approved by the Association. Ordination was always the prerogative of the local church, but only after examination and approval by the Association. Even before the American Revolution the Association encouraged the churches to be on the lookout for promising young men for the ministry, and also to establish schools for their education. Churches were also encouraged to maintain a high level of support for their ministers.[18]

Thirdly, the Association provided printed materials for the churches. Included in the standard publications were such items as a Confession of Faith, the Treatise of Discipline, a catechism, and a hymnal. Treatises were also published on baptism, apologetics, family worship, the education of children, and other subjects.

A fourth area of concern by the Association was missions. The Philadelphia Association began by sending missionaries into Virginia as early as 1745, and set up a fund for missionary support in 1750. By 1772 the Association had taken the responsibility of supporting work among the western tribes of Indians. With news of William Carey's missionary activities, the Association in 1794 empowered William Rogers to collect funds for "the propagation of the gospel among the Hindus." Not only did they help support home and overseas missions, but also gave to assist destitute churches, education, and widow's relief.[19]

A fifth concern of the Association was theological stability. When a church deviated from the accepted Confession of Faith, the Association stepped in to give a ruling. For example, in 1748 the Minutes of the Philadelphia Association indicate a censure was requested for those who denied the foreknowledge of God.[20] Also, in 1784, a church admitting unbaptized persons to the Lord's Table was the recipient of letters from sister churches exhorting a discontinuance of the practice. The letters were sent on the request of the Association.[21]

Finally, the Association assisted local churches in solving various types of problems, and also spoke out on political and social issues. By and large, the Associations encouraged the churches to seek solutions to problems within their own fellowship; failing in this, they should consult with the Association. The Associations also provided the Baptists a means of speaking and acting in unity on such matters as religious liberty, separation of church and state, slavery, and the use of intoxicating beverages.

From this brief survey of Baptist associational life it is evident that our Baptist forebears did not believe in or practice "local autonomy." The term "local autonomy" came into use in the nineteenth century to define "self-rule," and our modern use of the term implies more independence than was originally claimed. While jealously protecting the local church and its church power as a full and complete expression of the church of Christ, they also gave rightful place and authority to the universal church as expressed in the life of the Association.

There is a tension evident throughout Baptist history as they sought to give proper emphasis to the local church and the universal church. While it is true that the early Baptists tried to express their concept of the universal church in the Associational principle, it is also true they were not confronted by the many larger responsibilities of the Baptists of the nineteenth century.

By the time of the nineteenth century the tendency towards individualism and particularism led toward an overemphasis upon that facet of the Baptist concept of the church to the neglect of the other. Eventually the view of the universal church was forgotten. It would appear then that one of the responsibilities of present-day Baptists is to recognize that their real tradition offers to them a foundation for building a more coordinated convention life without the loss of local autonomy to a centralized bureauracy. Therefore, in the light of the above survey of Baptist associational life in the eighteenth century, the question must be asked, "What factors brought about the weakening of the associational life after such a strong beginning?"

Four

The Breakdown of Associational Life

There were two factors which began the process of weakening the place of the Association in Baptist life; namely, a fear of centralized power and a strong individualism which cultivated that fear. By the closing years of the eighteenth century, the Baptists were realizing the need for some type of national organization. New churches were springing up all over the country, along with new associations built upon the plan of the Philadelphia Association. The development of the new associations brought about the decline of the Philadelphia Association as a "national" organization. During the last decades of the eighteenth century, several suggestions were offered to provide Baptists with a plan for national cooperation.

One of the earliest plans offered came from Morgan Edwards, pastor of the First Baptist Church, Philadelphia, and an early Baptist historian. In 1770 he proposed that all new associations might be incorporated in the Philadelphia Association and thus create a national body for Baptists from Nova Scotia to Georgia. The Baptists of New England rejected this plan as too radical, fearing associational domination.[1] These Baptists were still plagued by the presence and pressure of the Established Church, and they saw in the growth of the Associations a foreboding of ecclesiastical domination. Their solution to the problem was the adoption of the society method of organization.

The society method brought together individual Baptists and churches as voluntary members of a society for a common purpose—in most cases missions. Among the Baptists the society method began in 1802 with the formation of the Massachusetts Domestic Missionary Society. Membership was open to anyone, regardless of denomination, for the minimum gift of one dollar per year. Up to one-third of the trustees could be non-Baptists, and no doctrinal standards were set up for the workers. As the nation expanded westward and the need for home mission work grew, other societies were formed in Maine in 1804, New York in 1805-07, Connecticut in 1809, and New Jersey in 1811. The reasons for the transition from the associational method to the society method were not difficult to understand.

In the first place Baptists had undoubtedly been influenced by the many missionary societies of England and Europe. Secondly, the society method was also in practice among other Protestant groups in America. Finally, some

Baptists feared a centralized authority embodied in the associations as they grew in number, strength, activity, and authority. Rather than face the problem of growing associational strength, the Baptists by-passed it by adopting the society method. Such a fear of centralized authority was fostered by a growing spirit of individualism in the new nation.

By the turn of the nineteenth century the emphasis in Baptist organizational life had shifted from seeking to discern the will of God to theological individualism and the freedom of the local church from ecclesiastical control. The theological individualism became known as "soul competency," and the freedom of the local church ultimately developed the title of "local autonomy." Perhaps no other person was so representative of this emerging viewpoint as Isaac Backus of New England.

In the viewpoint of Isaac Backus the local church was the complete expression of the church of Christ, and associations were optional and advisory. Backus had suffered much from and fought courageously against the Establishment in New England. In his theology, the fundamental relationship was between God and the person elected to salvation. Into this sphere neither church nor state may intrude. In his concept of the church Backus believed the local church was composed of individual believers, all competent to discern the will of God. Hence the local church was in all ways competent to govern itself. Sister churches *may* be called in to assist and advise in situations of ordaining and censuring. Backus opposed the initial effort to organize the Warren Association in Rhode Island along the lines of the Philadelphia Association. He later joined upon assurance contained in a revised plan of organization that the association "be no other than an advisory council." Backus's support of the association was also based on his recognition that it would be an effective instrument in the cause of Baptist freedom on state and national levels. However, the individualism of Isaac Backus was mild compared to his contemporary, John Leland, a Baptist preacher in Virginia.

In his concept of the church John Leland appears to have been influenced more by John Locke and Thomas Jefferson than by the New Testament. He stated:

> And it must be confessed, that the spirit and rule by which the subjects of Christ's kingdom are to live one among the other, greatly resemble the genius of a republic, and as greatly confronts the inequality and haughtiness of the monarchies.[2]

Leland argues for church government in the same vein Thomas Jefferson argued for political government; namely, "That government is best which governs least." Leland saw the association only as a means of fellowship and mutual encouragement. His position allowed no room for associational activity, even in the cause of missions. Yet it was for the very cause of missions that Baptists finally organized themselves on a national level.

In May of 1814 Baptists throughout the country agreed to meet together in Philadelphia for the purpose of forming a national missionary society. The name of the new society was "The General Missionary Convention of the Baptist Denomination in the United States for Foreign Missions." However, it became known later as the Triennial Convention because it met every three years. Following the trend already established, membership was limited to two delegates from each local and state missionary society or other religious body that contributed at least one hundred dollars per year. It was at the first meeting that Luther Rice and Adoniram Judson were appointed missionaries by the Board of Convention. By 1817 home missions and education had also become the responsibility of the Convention. However, it became increasingly evident that the Triennial Convention could not meet the needs of Baptist work on a national scale.

The natural solution to the problem lay in the extension of the associational principle to the state and national levels. The basic pattern was to bring the Associations together in the State Conventions, and then the State Conventions in the General Convention. In 1821 the first State Conventions were formed in South Carolina and New York. The State Conventions were formed of delegates from the Associations rather than the churches. Within two years similar Conventions were organized in Georgia and Alabama, with Vermont, Maine, Massachusetts, Virginia, and Mississippi in 1824.[3] The response to the emerging pattern from all sections of the country was enthusiastic. In 1823 the Triennial Convention urged the continuation of efforts to create State Conventions. Luther Rice, by this time a national Baptist leader, was encouraging the Triennial Convention to transform itself into a General Convention at its next meeting in 1826. However, the dreams for a national convention which seemed so certain of coming true never became a reality.[4]

The collapse of the movement to organize a General Convention of Baptists was brought about, in the main, by the volunteer missionary society. In 1825, a union of the New York State Convention with the Hamilton Baptist Missionary Society of New York was consummated. Ostensibly the merger was effected to avoid duplication of effort. However, the resultant organization was a missionary society rather a state convention. The action transformed the Associations from an important expression of the church of Christ to auxiliary missionary societies. By the time of the 1826 Triennial Convention the New York Society group had joined forces with the society interests of Massachusetts to control the Convention.[5]

With almost two thirds of the votes, the delegates from the two northern states proceeded to discredit Luther Rice, severed Columbian College from the Convention, and revised the constitution to limit Convention responsibility. It would be of value to discredit Luther Rice because of his leadership of the movement toward a General Convention. The unethical actions used in obtaining a censure of Rice has left a scar upon the face of Baptist history. In the minds of the New York delegates Columbian College was in competition with their theological seminary at Hamilton, New York. The Massachusetts Baptists had also established a seminary at Newton, Massachusetts. With the censure of Luther Rice an accomplished fact, the dissolution of the relationship with Columbian College, with which Rice was associated, was an easy step. The death blow to the possibility of a General Convention was in the form of a revision of the constitution limiting the responsibility of the Convention to foreign missions on the basis of voluntary support.[6] Standing in the vanguard of the forces which brought the General Convention movement to a halt was a prominent Baptist leader by the name of Francis Wayland.

Because of his prominence among Baptists over an extended period of time, Francis Wayland was one of the great influences in the nineteenth century for the development of the concept of "local autonomy." In the first place, over the period of his lifetime of active service he occupied positions of prominence as editor of two Baptist periodicals; as a leading board member of several missionary societies; in several offices of the Triennial Convention; as a board member of Newton Theological Institution; and as president of Brown University. Secondly, it was Wayland's leadership in bringing about the constitutional changes at the Triennial Conventions of 1826 and 1846 which dashed all hopes for a strong denomination. Finally, his influence was extended beyond his lifetime with the publication through five editions of his manual entitled "Notes on the Principles and Practices of Baptist Churches." Thus, through his extensive participation in Baptist life, Wayland's excessive individualism was able to penetrate deeply into the consciousness of Baptists even to the present day.

Wayland's view of the church and all associations was

predicated upon his extreme individualism. In his *Elements of Moral Science* he wrote, "Every human being is, by constitution, a separate and distinct, and complete system. . . . The possession of these (body, understanding, conscience and will) renders every human being a distinct and independent individual."[7] He believed the church was composed of regenerate individuals who were automatically rendered morally and spiritually competent by such a conversion experience. An individual exercises his right of private judgment when he joins a church with views similar to his own.

Wayland was committed to a course of absolute independency for the local church because of a naive view of the New Testament church and his seeming ignorance of Baptist history.[8] He saw the sole work of the church as the "conversion of souls," which required no organization beyond the local church. While he posed no objections to voluntary organizations for the mutual edification of the churches, they were not to engage in united activities. Furthermore, an association could not be composed of representatives of churches despite the plain facts of Baptist history. Wayland's unfortunate influence upon the course of Baptist thought in the first half of the nineteenth century was equaled by the influence of Landmarkism in the latter half.

Landmarkism is a descriptive term among Baptists of a concept of the church which sought to set up what was thought to be the marks of a New Testament church. These "Old Landmarks" were principles by which it was thought possible to trace the existence of all true Baptist churches back to the New Testament, and a church history was published to demonstrate this belief.[9] The movement was founded by Dr. James R. Graves who was editor of the *Tennessee Baptist* from 1846 until his death in 1893.[10] There were two basic ideas in Graves's concept of the church: (1) Because only Baptist churches can be traced back to the New Testament they alone have the right to baptize and ordain. (2) The Lord's Supper was only to be administered by the local church and only to believers baptized by immersion.[11]

An understanding of Landmarkism begins with its fundamental tenet, namely the primacy of the local church.[12] Graves believed that a true church was known by its practice of true baptism. Since only Baptist churches practiced New Testament baptism in unbroken succession from the time of the apostles, they alone were the true churches. He identified the Kingdom of God with the church and thus the Kingdom encompassed the churches; and the churches constitute the kingdom. The Landmarkist maintained that the New Testament word for church, *ecclēsia,* was used exclusively for the local church. However, an examination of the use of the word in the New Testament does not support such a view.

In the New Testament the word *ecclēsia* is used interchangeably for the local congregation and the whole church of Christ.[13] An example of this dual use of the word is found in Matthew, the only Gospel to use *ecclēsia.* Acts and the Pauline epistles also use the word in both senses. In Matthew 16:18 and 18:17 are found the only occasions when the word is used in the four Gospels. In the former it evidently refers to the whole church, while the latter seems to point to the local church. In Acts, the word is used many times.

In the book of Acts the early examples of the interchangeable use of the word are found in 2:47; 5:11; 8:1; 9:30. These references include one which localized the church at Jerusalem to the plural use in 9:31. Later references include the church at Jerusalem (11:22; 12:1,5; 15:4,22), the church at Antioch in Syria (11:26; 13:1; 14:27; 15:3), at Caesarea-Phillippi (18:22), and at Ephesus (20:17,28). To emphasize the localization in these references is to miss the main idea. The emphasis is not upon the locale of the church, but upon the church in a given locale. The frequent interchangeable use of the singular and the plural demonstrate this point. The *ecclēsia* (singular) is not divided up into *ecclēsiai* (plural) nor is *ecclēsia* formed by the coming together of the *ecclēsiai*. Rather it means that the church (*ecclēsia*) is present in a certain place.[14] Such a concept may also be seen in the writings of Paul.

While there are many localized uses of *ecclēsia* in the Pauline epistles (Romans 16:1; 1 Corinthians 1:2; II Corinthians 1:1; Colossians 4:16; I Thessalonians 1:1; II Thessalonians 1:1; *et al.*), it is also evident that Paul considered the local churches as expressions of the whole church. For example in I Corinthians 1:2 and II Corinthians 1:1 he does not address "the Corinthian church", but "the church as it is at Corinth." Furthermore, by the use of symbolic language the New Testament presents a picture of the church in both its universal and local understandings.

The New Testament uses several terms to portray the nature of the church. For example the church is the people of God (I Peter 2:9-10), the temple of God (I Corinthians 3:16-17), the body of Christ (I Corinthians 12:27-31), the bride of Christ (Ephesians 5:21-27), and the fellowship of the Holy Spirit (Phillippians 2:1). To limit these rich terms to the local church is to rob them of much meaning and importance. Such limited use raises some serious questions. Does God have several holy nations or one holy nation? Does He have one holy temple or many holy temples? To limit the church to the local church is to give Christ many brides rather than one bride; many bodies instead of one body. Does the New Testament emphasize Christ as the glorified head of the churches or the church? Does Paul speak of fellowship in *a* body of Christ or *the* body of Christ? The New Testament does not support a view of the church which excludes either its local or universal manifestations. "Rigid distinctions between the local assembly, especially when the general assembly as the body of Christ is rejected, is a case of not being able to see the woods for the trees."[15] Furthermore the New Testament picture of the church has several clear implications.

The Scriptures present a clearly defined relationship

between the parts and the whole of the church. If American Baptists, Southern Baptists or National Baptists say, "I am not of the body," are they therefore not a part of the body? If one Christian group says to another, "You are not a part of the body," is it therefore not a part of the body? Or can any Christian group say of itself, "We alone are the body"? The importance of the relationship between the church local and the church universal has been expressed by the saintly Dr. W. O. Carver:

> No local church and no denomination can come into the fulness of Christ's fellowship and experience without relating itself in its thoughts, its prayers, and its plans to all the saints who see the kingdom of God as the realm into which men are brought through the second birth by the working of the Holy Spirit.[16]

Furthermore, the New Testament recognizes the necessity for organization if the church is to fulfill its divine purpose. Hence gifts were given and offices created to facilitate the work of the church (Romans 12:3-8; I Corinthians 12:27-30; Ephesians 4:11-12). Such gifts were exercised in and through the local congregations because they were local expressions of the one universal church. However, this does not imply that organization and gifts are not essential on a broader scale. The same divine purpose exists for the whole church and the congregations. What is true for the whole church is true for the local churches. For example the divine commission was given to the whole church and is therefore the divine commission for all the churches. It is evident in the New Testament that gifts and offices were utilized to carry out the commission. Thus it can be seen that the nature of the church on a local level is more than spiritual because it assumes organizational and institutional forms. It naturally follows that organizational and institutional forms on a wider scale are just as Scriptural since the same purpose holds true for the whole church as well as the local churches. Thus does it appear that the Scriptures do not support the wholly localized concept of the church maintained by the Landmarkists. The influence of the Landmarkists among Southern Baptists has been extensive and only a little less so among the Baptists of the North.

The Landmarkists influence in the North was chiefly through Dr. James M. Pendleton. Although Pendleton was not as controversial a figure as Graves, he nonetheless exerted considerable influence as a founding trustee of Crozer Theological Seminary, in a long pastorate of the Upland Baptist Church in Pennsylvania, and as a manager of the American Baptist Publication Society. He wrote several books, including the widely read, *An Old Landmark Re-Set*. The influence of Landmarkism in the Southern Convention has been outlined by Dr. John E. Steely of Southeastern Baptist Seminary:

> It may be seen today in the changes in the nature of the Convention itself, both in fact and in the popular opinion; in the virtual identification of the kingdom of God and the visible church (with necessary elimination of *ecclēsia*); in the insistence of historical succession of Baptist churches since apostolic days; and in the emphasis of a high-church ecclesiology, as in the discussion of "alien immersion," "open communion," and the validity of certain ordinations. The objections on the part of some Baptists to being classified as Protestants also shows this influence.[17]

Two other factors promoting the concept of local autonomy among nineteenth-century Baptists were the New Hampshire Declaration of Faith and a flood of manuals, each purporting to teach historic Baptist principles and practice. The New Hampshire Declaration of Faith was published by the New Hampshire Baptist Convention in 1833, and defined the church only in terms of the local group of baptized believers. One of the co-authors, John

Newton Brown, was later book editor of the American Baptist Publication Society, and on his own authority had the New Hampshire Declaration published in *A Baptist Manual.* The Declaration was also incorporated in J. M. Pendleton's *Church Manual* and *The New Directory* by Hiscox. Because the New Hampshire Declaration of Faith defined the church exclusively in terms of the local church, it found ready acceptance by the Landmarkists and later the General Association of Regular Baptist Churches. With the addition of ten new sections Southern Baptists published the Declaration as an expression of their faith in 1925.

While many Baptist manuals were published in the nineteenth century the most popular by far was *The New Directory for Baptist Churches* by Edward T. Hiscox. The book was first published in 1859 and within thirty-five years had sold 60,000 copies and been translated into seven different languages for use by American Baptist missionaries. Hiscox strongly affirmed his belief in the absolute independency of the local church when he said, "Baptists assert that each particular local church is self-governing, and independent of *all other churches,* and of all the administration of its own affairs." An association is a voluntary body and not a representative body since "a Baptist Church cannot be represented by delegates authorized to act for it in any other organization whatsoever."[18] Similar expressions are found in D. C. Haynes's *The Baptist Denomination* (1856), Francis Wayland's *Principles and Practices of Baptist Churches* (1857), J. M. Pendleton's *Church Manual* (1867), H. Harvey's *The Church: Its Polity and Ordinances* (1879), and E. C. Dargan's *Ecclesiology* (1897).

In retrospect it may be seen that the Baptists of the nineteenth century exchanged a concept of the church which was both catholic and congregational for the dwarfed and distorted concept of local autonomy. For a period of approximately seventy-five years the associational principle was subjected to constant bombardment by persons and movements obsessed with a zeal without knowledge of the Baptist concept of the church. The artillery employed in destroying the citadel of the association was the spoken word, the written word, convention politics, and influential leadership. By such means were Baptists conditioned into accepting a concept of the church which was based on the misinterpretation of Scripture and a misrepresentation of Baptist history. Baptists remained practically undisturbed in their firm adherence to the "splendid isolation" concept of the local church until well into the twentieth century before voices were heard questioning its validity as Baptist doctrine.

Five

The Changing Scene in the Twentieth Century

By the last decade of the nineteenth century, Baptists in the North were becoming aware of the inadequacy of their pattern of organization in cooperative work. For almost one hundred years the doctrine of "local autonomy" had been the paramount concern in the Baptist view of the church. For the same period of time the voluntary society with a monetary basis for membership was the means of cooperative endeavor. As the needs for Baptist work multiplied so also did the number of societies with the organization of the Foreign Mission Society in 1814, the Publication Society in 1824, the Home Mission Society in 1832, the Women's Home Mission in 1877, and the Women's Foreign Mission Society in 1913. However, there was virtually no coordination between the societies, and the churches were continually beseiged with agents of the societies with pleas for financial support.[1] In an effort to correct this awkward situation Northern Baptists began making moves in the last decade of the nineteenth century which ultimately led to the organization of the Northern Baptist Convention.

By 1896 the American Baptist Missionary Union, the

American Baptist Home Mission Society, and the American Baptist Publication Society brought about the creation of the Commission on Systematic Beneficence to avoid the duplication of appeals for financial support. In 1901 a Commission on Coordination made further recommendations for closer working relationships between the societies.[2] Finally, in 1907, a general meeting of all the three societies previously named met on May 16-17 in Washington, D.C. to set up the organization of the Northern Baptist Convention. However, the records reveal an apprehension over the growing connectionalism embodied in the organization of a national body.[3]

In the organization of the Northern Baptist Convention special pains were taken to safeguard the independence of the local churches, the cooperating organizations, and the affiliated agencies. At the organizational meeting the representatives, declared their "belief in the independency of the local church, in the advisory and representative nature of the local and state associations, . . ."[4] Furthermore the cooperating agencies were to retain their legal independence and could withdraw membership upon one year's notice.[5] These built-in safeguards to protect independence only served to accentuate the polarity in Baptist thought about the church.

On the one hand there was a recognizable need for efficiency in the broader relationships, but there was also the desire to retain "local autonomy." In the process of seeking to resolve the polarity by the creation of a convention they seemed to have overlooked the theological questions involved and failed to recognize the need for a balanced view of the church. The organization of the convention was motivated by practical purposes rather than a theological concern for expressing a true Baptist concept of the church. As stated in the Act of Incorporation the object was to provide a sounding board for Baptist opinions, a means of cooperating in missions, and a more efficient system of fund raising.[6] However, in several areas of Baptist life there were some expressions of a more balanced view of the church. Typical of these expressions were those of Henry G. Weston of Crozer Theological Seminary and August H. Strong of Rochester Theological Seminary.

The church for Weston was both the "whole body of believers in Christ" and a "body of professed believers in Christ . . . associated for worship, work and discipline."[7] Strong took several steps closer to a more historical Baptist view of the church, for he saw the church as "nothing less than the body of Christ—the organism to which he gives spiritual life, and through which he manifests his power and grace."[8] Though he recognized the local church as the ultimate ecclesiastical authority, Strong described it as a "smaller company of regenerate persons, who, in any community, unite themselves voluntarily together in accordance with Christ's laws, for the complete establishment of His kingdom in themselves and in the world."[9] However, views such as those held by Weston and Strong found little acceptance in Baptist thought during this period. Furthermore the creation of the new Convention did little to resolve the polarity between the desire for efficiency and the desire to protect autonomy.

Because the organization of the Northern Baptist Convention had failed to close the gap between operational efficiency and local autonomy a long process of reorganization began by the end of the first decade of Convention history. In 1918 a Committee of five laymen was appointed to plan a more efficient organization. The results of the Committee's recommendations led to several changes. In 1920 a Board of General Promotion was created to make an annual review of the work of the Convention, and to prepare plans and a budget for the ensuing year. In 1924 the name of the agency was changed to The Board of Missionary Cooperation, and for ten years carried the burden of promoting the Convention program.[10] In 1925 a professional research firm submitted a report with recommendations for strengthening the Convention structure. A few of the suggestions were adopted, but most of them were set aside."[11] In 1934 a Commission of Fifteen recommended a Council on Finance and Promotion to replace the Board of Missionary Cooperation. It also recommended the creation of a General Council to replace the Executive Committee. The new General Council was given wide powers in the administration of the Convention.[12] The process of reorganization continued with the appointment of a Commission of Review in 1947 "to make a general study of our denomination between now and the year 1950." Several changes grew out of the acceptance of the Commission's report including the appointment of a General Secretary. Studies of the Convention's organizational problems were initiated by the new General Secretary, Dr. Reuben Nelson. In 1956 the General Council submitted a plan of reorganization to the Convention at Seattle, but several years passed before a plan was adopted in 1961.[13] Following the adoption of the plan of reorganization the Convention set in motion machinery geared to determine the value and effectiveness of area promotional agencies called the SAAR Project (Study of Administrative Areas and Relationships). Still later a Study Commission on Denominational Structure (SCODS) was created for the possibility of still further changes. Both of these projects will be given a more complete treatment later in the book, but this brief resumé demonstrates a cardinal issue. Northern Baptists have had great difficulty resolving the polarity between their desires to achieve efficiency and retain local autonomy. Each change in the structure has been accompanied by expressed fears of growing centralization and a concern for the continuance of "local autonomy." However, Southern Baptists have not been without their problems related to the emphasis on local autonomy since creating their Convention in 1845.

With the organization of the Southern Baptist Convention there was a change from the society method to the denominational method of caring for responsibilities in missions, education and publication, but the financial basis for membership continued for almost another one hundred years. Finally, the Convention became a denomination in a true sense in that it became a convention of churches. However, with the Landmark emphasis upon the local church to the exclusion of the universal church several problems soon arose. W. E. Barnes has suggested that the primacy of the local church in Landmarkism gave birth to four distinct controversies in the Southern Convention.

> Landmarkism claimed that the local church had the ultimate authority over the proclamation of the gospel (nonpulpit affiliation); over the ordinances of the gospel (anti-alien immersion and church communion); over the method of the proclamation of the gospel (anti-convention and anti-board). The fourth phase expressed itself in the sphere of history. The taproot of high churchism is historical continuity. If the local church could not be traced to the first century then the very life of Landmarkism was endangered.[14]

At the heart of each controversy, expressed in one form or another, was the ever present emphasis on "local autonomy." The problem over the proclamation of the gospel revolved around the question of whether or not ministers of non-Baptist churches were true ministers. Since only Baptist churches were true churches the ministers of such other churches were not true ministers. With such reasoning did the Landmarkists begin a major controversy in 1855. However, this dispute soon spread to the matter of the administration of the ordinances. The Landmarkists claimed that "the members of no one church have a right to come to the table in another church, though of the same faith and order; for each church is independent.[15] While the matter of ordinances stirred warm debate before and after the Civil War it was not until the controversy over missions that the life of the Convention was really endangered.

The dispute over missions was twofold, namely the ques-

tion of administration and method in missions. Right at the
center of the storm was the emphasis on the autonomy of the
local church. The Landmarkists contended that missions
should not be the responsibility of a board, but of local
churches. Beginning in 1859 they made several efforts to
change the character of the Southern Convention from a
membership based on interest and financial support to one
of churches, but without success. The efforts were renewed
in 1869, 1874, 1891, and in 1895. The question of missionary
methods also involved the primacy of the local church.
Basically the "Gospel Missionism" dispute involved the
application of Landmark principles to the foreign-mission
field. Dr. T. P. Crawford and others of like mind insisted
at the 1888 convention that native Christianity be self-sup-
porting and self-controlling from the very beginning. Thus
they opposed definite salary commitments to missionaries
and any borrowing to support them, further obviating the
necessity for boards. While "Gospel Missionism" stirred
considerable dispute in the 1880s and 1890s it began to
weaken by the turn of the century. Landmarkism had also
spent much of its immediate force after fifty years, but not
before many of the extremists withdrew to form their own
organization.[16]

Finally the matter of the succession of local churches
came to the fore in the Whitsitt Controversy. The dispute
broke out in 1896 when Dr. William H. Whitsitt, president
of Southern Seminary, placed present day Baptist beginnings with the Congregationalists of seventeenth-century
England. Such a concept brought on open conflict with
Landmark views and Dr. Whitsitt ultimately resigned. While
the twentieth century has seen the Southern Convention
enjoy a period of unparalleled growth and unity it is still
beset with problems growing out of its ecclesiology.[17] Even
after the turn of the century several influences served to
help keep alive the exaggerated emphasis upon the local
church.

Through the first four decades of the twentieth century

several widely used sources still advocated the nineteenth-century concept of "local autonomy." *The New Directory For Baptist Churches* by Hiscox was still getting wide circulation as was E. Y. Mullins's *Axioms of Religion*. Here again Baptist organizational life beyond the local church was described as voluntary, and for advisory and administrative purposes only.[18] Two other notable examples were manuals on Baptist polity by William R. McNutt of Crozer Theological Seminary and H. E. Dana of Central Baptist Theological Seminary.

McNutt had what he called "two doctrinal strata" which were "soul competency" and the "free association of believers." In McNutt's thought "soul competency" was the "creative idea that the individual is competent in all matters of religion; has within himself by divine gift and right those capacities that make him competent to meet all the demands with which genuine religion confronts him; . . . he is able to make his own approach to God."[19] Such competent people freely associate themselves together to form a local competent church, independent and democratic.[20] Thus McNutt pictured the church as a group of individuals who considered themselves competent in religion and joined together for the furtherance of their own purposes.[21] McNutt appears to be suggesting an ecclesiastical humanism.

H. E. Dana followed a curious pattern of philological sidestepping in order to demonstrate that the word *ecclēsia* in the New Testament refers exclusively to a local congregation. Baptist churches were "each a complete and independent unit within itself." The congregationalism of the Baptists was a reproduction of the New Testament church, and at the center of it all was the local church, absolutely sovereign and independent. The local church was to have "no organic relation to any other church or governing assembly of representatives from local churches."[22] However, by the fourth decade it was possible to detect a changing pattern in Baptist thought about the church.

Six

Recovery in These Latter Days

In recent years a changing pattern in Baptist thought about the church has been taking place in England and the United States. Renewed study of the church by all Baptist groups has led us to see our uncritical approach to the church. These emerging patterns are defining the church with a more balanced understanding of its local and universal character. In England it was H. Wheeler Robinson in 1946 who defined the Church as a "society divinely controlled and implicitly on the assumption that the 'Congregational polity' here stated is adequate to the divine control."[1] In 1946 Robert Walton's *Gathered Community* defined the church in terms of a divine community rather than a voluntary society of individuals. Concerning the association he said:

> The principles we have inherited do not permit of any compulsory association of churches, or any authority imposed from above, but they do permit the extension of the principle of voluntary association to its furthest limits, even to the free acceptance of the authority of those whom the churches choose to serve them.[2]

In 1952 Ernest Payne also pointed out that "Baptists have regarded the visible church as finding expression in local communities of believers . . . , and who find an extension and expression of their life in free association, . . . with other churches of their own faith and order.[3]

In the United States, Baptists were rethinking their concepts of the Church in theological conferences. Perhaps two of the most significant symposiums coming out of the Baptist theological conferences were *What Is the Church* edited by

Duke K. McCall of the Southern Baptist Convention, and *Baptist Concepts of the Church* edited by Winthrop S. Hudson of the American Baptist Convention. In the introduction to *What Is the Church,* W. O. Carver set the direction of the book by speaking of the congregation "as a local manifestation of the church, begins in and follows from, the fact that the total body of the redeemed constitutes the continuing growing body of Christ."[4] The American Baptist volume traced the pattern of Baptist thought and action with reference to the church from the founding of the Philadelphia Association to the twentieth century. The clear perspective of the series of papers is a view of the process by which Baptists had moved away from their original concepts of the church. Several factors have prompted the emergence of a more Biblical and historical Baptist view of the church.

In the first place the problem of the wholesale defection of churches from the American Baptist Convention as the result of the theological controversies in the twentieth century has pointed up a basic weakness in the "local autonomy" concept; namely, the inability to maintain unity among Baptists. Secondly, the continuing process of centralization growing out of a desire for good stewardship and efficiency in a day of rising costs is giving some Baptists "heart tremors" over the future status of the local church. Thirdly, it is evident that efficiency of operation in itself is not an adequate basis for a national Baptist organization. Baptist organizational life beyond the local church has yet to be given a theological foundation. In the fourth place, the growing spirit of unity expressed in the Baptist World Alliance and North American Baptist Fellowship as well as some involvements in the Ecumenical Movement is challenging Baptists to reexamine their view of the church. Finally, the resurgence of interest in theology has helped create a climate favorable to a critical examination of some of our cherished concepts. Not only has the new interest in the church among Baptists developed because of these several factors, but it has also pointed up a number problems.

Perhaps the chief problem is the inability of Baptists to develop an adequate view of the whole church of Christ. Under the "local autonomy" view of the church, God has several holy temples, and Christ has many bodies and brides. Baptists have reversed the order of their forebears in their view of the church. Seventeenth-century Baptists began with a view of the whole church and then defined the local church as an agency by which the whole church functioned in a given geographic area. Because present-day Baptists begin with the local church and claim too much for it, they cannot develop an adequate concept of the whole church.

A second problem has been the erosion of Baptist fellowship and strength through the practice of defection by local churches. Concomitant with this problem is the inability of the association or the convention to enforce ministerial standards for the protection of the local churches against ministers who would foster a spirit of dissension.

In the third place, Baptists have the problem of justifying the continued existence of the association. In present Baptist practice the association is one in name only and serves only as an annual meeting. Because the association no longer serves its true purpose, the local churches no longer possess an effective means of directing Baptist affairs beyond the local church. Congregations cannot determine and direct Baptist policy and program through the national conventions because the national bodies are too large for deliberative purposes. Perhaps the most incisive analysis of this problem is contained in the book *Authority and Power In the Free Church Tradition* by Paul Harrison.

In the first place Harrison contends that the doctrine of "local autonomy" is a violation of the doctrine of the sovereignty of God and the freedom of the Holy Spirit.[5] Since "local autonomy" is but a wider circle around "soul competency" emphasis is made upon man rather than God. Harrison has discovered the earlier Baptist concept that freedom was not an end in itself, but a means toward understanding the mind of the Holy Spirit.

Secondly, Harrison claims that the actual organization and operation of the American Baptist Convention is inconsistent with the Baptist doctrine of the church.[6] The role of the professional leader is not sharply defined and as a result the agency heads increase the area of their power by extending the area of the activity of their agency. Any effort to bring Baptist practice in line with Baptist doctrine is usually the outgrowth of practical considerations such as efficiency rather than a Baptist theology of the church.[7] Harrison's contention of this point is aptly illustrated by the use of a secular research firm to recommend a pattern of reorganization of the Convention for more efficient operation.[8]

Fourthly, because of the state of "theological anarchy" which exists among Baptists, they have been unable to produce a confession of their faith that speaks to our modern world. The "old chestnut" of finding three opinions among two Baptists would be laughable if it were not so tragically true. If two Baptists do manage to agree, they will not give expression to their belief because many of them have been conditioned to think that Baptists do not believe in confessions of faith. While it is not possible to find simple solutions to complex problems, it is possible to offer some guidelines for the future, and to point out those visible signs of recovery in present Baptist life.

If Baptists are to discard their present truncated concept of the church for one which is both catholic and congregational, a process of education appears to be of prime importance. This process may take place in several areas, and fortunately has already begun. Our Baptist historians and theologians are expanding their efforts through study, research, and writing to promulgate a more accurate interpretation of Baptist history and polity. The fruit of their labors is still years removed from maturity in Baptist church life, but can be seen more immediately in the lives of their seminary students and recent graduates. Another phase of the reeducation process has been the availability of a new

Baptist manual which provides guidance and instruction
consistent with a true Baptist understanding of the church.[9]
Other manuals of similar quality are sure to follow.

The process of reeducation should be accompanied by a
reevaluation of the role of the Association in Baptist life.
Our traditional concept of the church would seem to require
that the Association be brought in from the circumference
of our Baptist organizational life. Again, as in the preceding
suggestion, several avenues are open to us. First and fore-
most it seems imperative that local churches will need to
balance their concept of freedom with a concept of responsibility in Associational relationships. By so doing we Baptists
would restore to the Association the strength and vitality it
must possess to be an expression of the church of Christ.
It would restore the power of discipline to the Association
and make possible the creation of effective standards for the
ministry. However, in order to bring such strength to the
Association it is essential that Baptists become once again a
confessional people. A new Baptist confession would define
the Baptist position, provide standards for organizational
life, and justify the existence of Baptists among other
Christian groups. One of the brightest rays of hope indi-
cating a recovery of the associational principle in the
American Baptist Convention is the SAAR Project.

In 1961 the Executive Secretaries of the State Conventions and City Societies requested the General Council of
the American Baptist Convention to initiate a study of
administrative areas and relationships. This project was
authorized and became known as the Study of Administrative Areas and Relationships. The twenty-member committee appointed for this project was charged with studying
the administrative procedures, groupings and relationships
within the American Baptist Convention. The purpose of
the SAAR Project has been stated:

Aside from the concern of whether it was good

stewardship to have fifty state conventions and city societies handling the administrative work and programming
for American Baptist congregations, an over-arching concern was that of working with our local congregations to
more effectively achieve the mission each has, in the
name of Jesus Christ. . . . Smaller groupings of congregations called areas, have been deemed more appropriate
units for developing of annual program emphases and
concerns by representatives of those congregations who
will actually do the program work.[10]

The implementation of the recommendations of the SAAR
Project has seen the creation of regions and areas which are
designed to help the local congregation achieve a more effective mission. It is all the churches working to help each other
in mission. To give the local congregation an even stronger
role on the national level a Study Commission on Denominational Structure was created.

The Study Commission on Denominational Structure
(SCODS) was created in 1968 and its 1971 report expressed
a balanced view of the church when in stating its responsibilities it said:

The responsibilities of the Commission were weighty.
They demanded adherence to traditional Baptist concepts of theology and polity, responsiveness to a world
in rapid change, commitment to working for maximum
participation of all Baptists within the life of the church,
and a structure firm enough to discourage provincialism,
parochialism and fragmentation while flexible enough to
encourage creativity and the possibility for the prophetic
voices to be heard.[11]

The basic recommendations of SCODS give further evidence of the emergence of a more balanced view of the

church. These recommendations were drawn up after a series of listening conferences all across the American Baptist Convention and they included changing the name of the national body from the American Baptist Convention to "American Baptist Churches." Thus there is an effort to recover our theological identity as a "churchly body" rather than that of annual meeting. The new name also emphasizes the change from a collection of societies to a national organization made up of the churches. The recommendations also provide for more adequate representation of the churches in the policy-making structure of the national organization. It would appear then that current events in Baptist life are moving toward a restoration of associational concepts even at a national level.

A national Baptist organization should have both a theological foundation and be representative in structure. An organizational structure based only on functional ability will eventually rob the local churches of their cherished freedom or result in complete withdrawal from all cooperative endeavor. The former would be tyranny and the latter would be tragedy. If our concept of the church holds that Christ is present with the believers wherever they gather, whether in a local congregation or deliberative assembly, then we must give credence to the proposition that the church does exist beyond the arena of the local church as well as within it. An acceptance of such an understanding of the church would make possible the creation of a *congregational pattern* of organization all the way up to the national level.

The creation of a national organization by Baptists along a congregational pattern would make possible the representation of the local Baptist church in national polity and program. Our Baptist forebears made it very clear that local churches were to send representatives or delegates to act on behalf of the churches they represented, and not on their own behalf. Therefore, it seems consistent with the Associational principle for the local churches to elect delegates to the Associations or Areas; the Associations or Areas to the State Conventions or Regional Conventions, and the State Conventions or Regions to the National Convention. While such a structure may seem to be more Presbyterian than Baptist, in actuality it is not. Any similarity would end at the point of the local church power it possesses. Such a pattern of organization would seem to have several benefits not now possible under our present set-up.

In the first place, local churches would again play an effective role in directing Baptist life because denominational leadership would hear the voices of the churches through their associations or areas. Secondly, the increasing exorbitant costs of national conventions would be reduced to release more money for local and benevolent purposes. Thirdly, it would discount the claim that mergers of Baptist conventions would result in too large and unwieldy an organization. In the fourth place, it would strengthen the Baptist witness, unity and fellowship on the Associational or Area level.

In the beginning of the nineteenth century Baptists were on their way to the promised land of bringing into being a visible expression of the church which was both Biblical and consistent with their own beliefs. However, for the past one hundred and fifty years they have wandered in a wilderness of a poor theology of the church. Here they have fallen prey to all sorts of enemies in the forms of organizational indecision, provincialism, and microscopic vision. Now, near the three-quarter mark of the twentieth century they stand at the brink of Jordan ready to cross over into Canaan. The old generation died in the wilderness, and a new generation of Baptists seems about to possess the land. The SAAR and SCODS Project are a stirring of the waters as they are about to part. If Baptists succeed in entering the promised land of a visible form of the church which is both Biblical and Baptist they will enjoy the milk and honey of an era of witness, worship, and fellowship beyond anything they have ever known.

Notes

CHAPTER ONE

1. Perry Miller, *Orthodoxy in Massachusetts*, p. 55.
2. William Haller, *The Rise of Puritanism*, p. 184.
3. Perry Miller, *Orthodoxy in Massachusetts*, p. 57.
4. Raymond P. Stearns, *Congregationalism in the Dutch Netherlands*, p. 4. (quoting from Jacob's "Four Assertions" in Benjamin Hanbury, Historical Memorials Relating to The Independents or Congregationists (3 vols. London 1839) I, 222).
5. *Ibid.*, pp. 5, 6.
6. Perry Miller, *Orthodoxy in Massachusetts*, p. 170.
7. Daniel Jenkins, *Congregationalism: A Restatement*, pp. 96-99.

CHAPTER TWO

1. Robert Torbet, *A History of the Baptists*, pp. 64-66.
2. *Ibid.*, p. 66.
3. Perry Miller, *Orthodoxy in Massachusetts*, p. 58.
4. William L. Lumpkin, *The Orthodox Confession of 1678*, pp. 285-289.
5. William L. Lumpkin, *Baptist Confessions of Faith*, p. 17.
6. William L. Lumpkin, *The Orthodox Confession of 1678*, p. 319.
7. Robert C. Walton, *The Gathered Community*, p. 84.

CHAPTER THREE

1. Winthrop Hudson, "The Associational Principle Among Baptists," *Foundations*, January 1958, p. 10.

2. Robert Handy, *Baptist Concepts of the Church,* ed. Winthrop Hudson (Philadelphia: The Judson Press, 1959), p. 31.

3. *Ibid.,* p. 32.

4. Robert Torbet, *A History of the Baptists,* p. 232.

5. William L. Lumpkin, *The Orthodox Confession of 1678,* pp. 352-353.

6. Edward T. Hiscox, *The New Directory for Baptist Churches,* p. 320.

7. Winthrop Hudson, *"The Associational Principle Among Baptists," Foundations,* January 1958, pp. 14-15.

8. *Ibid.,* p. 19.

9. *Ibid.,* pp. 19-20.

10. Benjamin Griffiths, *An Essay on the Power and Duty of the Association,* p. 62.

11. *Ibid.,* p. 62.

12. *Ibid.,* pp. 28-29.

13. John P. Gates, "The Association as it Affected Baptist Polity in North America," *The Chronicle,* January 1943, p. 21.

14. William L. Lumpkin, *The Orthodox Confession of 1678,* pp. 285-286.

15. Robert C. Walton, *The Gathered Community,* p. 11.

16. R. W. Kicklighter, *What Is The Church,* ed. Duke K. McCall (quoting from "The Origin of The Church"), p. 38.

17. Robert Torbet, *A History of the Baptists,* pp. 229-230.

18. Minutes of the Philadelphia Baptist Association, ed. A. D. Gillette (Philadelphia: American Baptist Publication Society, 1851), pp. 25, 27, 77, 86.

19. Winthrop Hudson, "The Associational Principle Among Baptists," *Foundations,* January 1958, p. 18.

20. John P. Gates, "The Association as it Affected Baptist Polity in North America," *The Chronicle,* January 1943, p. 24.

21. R. E. E. Harkness, "Early Practices of the Baptists in America," *The Chronicle,* January 1944, p. 15.

CHAPTER FOUR

1. Robert Torbet, "Baptist Thought About the Church," *Foundations,* April 1958, p. 26.

2. Edwin Gaustad, *Baptist Concepts of the Church,* p. 123. ed. Winthrop Hudson ("The Backus-Leland Tradition," quoted from L. T. Greene, ed. The Writings of John Leland. New York, 1845, 1. 275).

3. Winthrop Hudson, "Stumbling Into Disorder," *Foundations,* April 1958, p. 47.

4. *Ibid.,* p. 47.

5. *Ibid.,* pp. 48-49

6. *Ibid.,* pp. 48-58.

7. Norman Maring, *Baptist Concepts of the Church,* ed. Winthrop Hudson (Philadelphia: The Judson Press, 1959), p. 202.

8. *Ibid.,* pp. 153-167.

9. G. H. Orchard, *A Concise History of Foreign Baptists.*

10. Landmarkism, itself, is largely a product of New England Separatism as represented by Backus and Leland. Graves was also a native of New England. . . . *Historic Baptist Ecclesiology,* Doctoral Dissertation, Columbia University, N.Y., 1960): "Landmarkism may be said to have been the incursion into Southern Baptist Life, in which the Philadelphia ecclesiology has been the most prominent type, of the ecclesiology of New England separatism, engrafted upon a Baptist base" (p. 265).

11. Robert Torbet, "Baptist Thought About the Church," *Foundations,* April 1958, p. 30.

12. Robert Torbet, *Baptist Concepts of the Church,* ed. Winthrop Hudson (Philadelphia: The Judson Press, 1959), p. 179.

13. Carl Ludwig Schmidt, *The Church*, ed. Gerhard Kittel (New York: Harper Brothers, 1951), p. 9.

14. *Ibid.*, p. 7.

15. Dale Moody, *The Nature of the Church*, ed. Duke K. McCall (Nashville: Broadman Press, 1958), p. 18.

16. W. O. Carver, *What Is The Church*, p. 14.

17. John E. Steely, *What Is The Church*, ed. Duke K. McCall (Nashville: Broadman Press, 1958), p. 143.

18. Edward T. Hiscox, *The New Directory for Baptist Churches*, pp. 17, 335.

CHAPTER FIVE

1. Robert Torbet, *A History of the Baptists*, p. 453.

2. *Ibid.*, p. 453.

3. *A Manual of the Northern Baptist Convention*, 1908-1918. "Statement on Background of Proposed Reorganization of the American Baptist Convention, 1956," ed. W. C. Bitting (Philadelphia: American Baptist Publication Society), pp. 1-16.

4. *Ibid.*, p. 9.

5. *Ibid.*, p. 27.

6. *Ibid.*, p. 19.

7. Henry G. Weston, *Constitution and Polity of the New Testament Church*, pp. 17, 20.

8. Augustus H. Strong. *Systematic Theology*, p. 888.

9. *Ibid.*, p. 890.

10. Robert Torbet, *A History of the Baptists*, pp. 455-456.

11. Management Audit of the American Baptist Convention, N.Y., American Institute Management, 1955, p. 3.

12. Robert Torbet, *A History of the Baptists*, p. 456.

13. *A Manual of the Northern Baptist Convention*, 1908-1918. "Statement on Background of Proposed Reorganization of the American Baptist Convention, 1956," ed. W.C. Bitting (Philadelphia: American Baptist Publication Society).

14. W. W. Barnes. *The Southern Baptist Convention,* 1844-1953, pp. 105-106.

15. *Ibid.,* p. 107. (quoting from *The Tennessee Baptist,* September 1, 1855, Col. 1).

16. *Ibid.,* pp. 109-117.

17 John Steely, *What Is The Church,* ed. Duke K. McCall (quoting from "The Landmark Movement in The Southern Baptist Convention"), pp. 146-147.

18. E. Y. Mullins, *The Axioms of Religion,* p. 147.

19. William R. McNutt, *Polity and Practice of Baptist Churches,* p 21.

20. *Ibid.,* pp. 26-27.

21. *Ibid.,* pp. 27-31

22. H. E. Dana, *A Manual of Ecclesiology,* pp. 19, 104-105.

CHAPTER SIX

1. H. Wheeler Robinson, *The Life and Faith of the Baptists,* p. 83.

2. Robert C. Walton, *The Gathered Community,* pp. 112-125.

3. Ernest A. Payne, *The Fellowship of Believers,* p. 36.

4. W. O. Carver, *What Is the Church,* ed. Duke K. McCall, p. 7.

5 Paul M. Harrison, *Authority and Power in the Free Church Tradition,* p. 220.

6. *Ibid.,* pp. 13-14.

7. *Ibid.,* p. 217.

8. Management Audit of the American Baptist Convention, N.Y., American Institute of Management, 1955.

9. Norman Maring and Winthrop Hudson, *A Baptist Manual of Polity and Practice.*

10. Constitutional Convention Booklet, The American Baptist Churches of the Pacific Southwest, 1970.

11. Report of the Study Commission on Denominational structure, American Baptist Convention, 1971.

Bibliography

BOOKS

Atkins, G. A., and Fagley, F. L. *History of American Congregationalism.* Boston: The Pilgrim Press, 1942.

Backus, Isaac. *A History of New England.* Newton, 1871.

_____. *Church History of New England.* 1620-1804. Vol. II. Philadelphia: The American Baptist Publication Society, 1853.

Baker, Robert A. *Relations Between Northern and Southern Baptists.* Forth Worth: Seminary Hill Press, 1948.

Barnes, W. W. *The Southern Baptist Convention, 1844-1953.* Nashville: Broadman Press, 1954.

_____. *The Southern Baptist Convention, Study in the Development of Ecclesiology.* Fort Worth: Seminary Hill, 1934.

Bradford, Amory H. *The Pilgrim in Old New England.* London: James Clarke and Company, 1893.

Campolo, Anthony, Jr. *A Denomination Looks At Itself.* Valley Forge: Judson Press, 1971.

Cook, Henry. *What Baptists Stand For.* London: The Carey Kingsgate Press, 1958.

Crowell, William. *The Church Members Manual of Ecclesiastical Principles.* Boston: Gould and Lincoln, 1854.

Dagg, John L. *Church Order, A Treatise.* Philadelphia: The American Baptist Publication Society, 1858.

Dana, H. E. *A Manual of Ecclesiology.* Kansas City: Central Seminary Press, 1941.

Dargan, Edwin C. *Ecclesiology.* Louisville: Charles T. Dearing, 1897.

Edwards, Morgan. *Materials Toward a History of American Baptists.* Philadelphia, 1770-92, Vol. I.

————. *The Customs of Primitive Baptist Churches.* Philadelphia, 1768.

Forsyth, Peter T. *Faith, Freedom and the Future.* New York: Hodder and Stoughton.

Griffiths, Benjamin. *An Essay on the Power and Duty of the Association.* Philadelphia Baptist Association Minutes. 1749.

Hallen, William. *The Rise of Puritanism.* New York: Columbia University Press, 1958.

Harrison, Paul M. *Authority and Power in the Free Church Tradition.* Princeton: Princeton University Press, 1959.

Harvey, M. *The Church.* Philadelphia: The American Baptist Publication Society, 1879.

Haynes, D. C. *The Baptist Denomination.* New York: Sheldon Blakeman and Company, 1856.

Hiscox, Edward T. *The New Directory for Baptist Churches.* Philadelphia: American Baptist Publication Society, 1894.

Hudson, Winthrop S. (ed.) *Baptist Concepts of the Church.* Philadelphia: The Judson Press, 1959.

Jenkins, Daniel. *Congregationalism: A Restatement.* London: Faber and Faber, 1954.

Lumpkin, William L. *Baptist Confessions of Faith.* Philadelphia: The Judson Press, 1959.

Maring, Norman and Hudson, Winthrop. *A Baptist Manual of Polity and Practice.* Valley Forge: The Judson Press, 1963.

McCall, Duke K. (ed.) *What Is the Church.* Nashville: Broadman Press, 1958.

McNutt, William R. *Polity and Practice of Baptist Churches.* Philadelphia: The Judson Press, 1935.

Miller, Perry. *Orthodoxy in Massachusetts.* Cambridge: Harvard University Press, 1933.

Mullins, E. Y. *The Axioms of Religion.* Philadelphia: Griffith and Rowland Press, 1908.

_____. *Baptist Beliefs.* Philadelphia: The Judson Press, 1925.

Orchard, G. H. *A Concise History of Foreign Baptists.* Nashville: Tennessee Publication Society.

Payne, Ernest A. *The Free Church Tradition in the Life of England.* London: SCM Press, 1944.

_____. *The Fellowship of Believers.* London: The Carey Kingsgate Press, 1952.

Pendleton, J. M. *Church Manual.* Philadelphia: The American Baptist Publication Society, 1867.

_____. *Distinctive Principles of Baptists.* Philadelphia: American Baptist Publication Society, 1882.

Reynolds, J. L. *Church Polity.* Richmond: Harrold and Murray, 1849.

Robinson, H. Wheeler. *Baptist Principles.* London: The Carey Kingsgate Press, 1925.

_____. *The Life and Faith of the Baptists.* London: The Kingsgate Press, 1946.

Rouner, Arthur A. Jr. *The Congregational Way of Life.* Englewood Cliffs, N.J.: Prentice-Hall, Inc., 1960.

Shakespeare, J. H. *Baptist and Congregational Pioneers.* London: The Kingsgate Press, 1905.

Stearns, Raymond P. *Congregationalism in the Dutch Netherlands.* Chicago: The American Society of Church History, 1940

Strong, Augustus H. *Systematic Theology.* Philadelphia: The Judson Press, 1907.

Torbet, Robert. *A History of the Baptists.* Philadelphia: The Judson Press, 1950.

Vedder, Henry C. *A Short History of Baptists.* Philadelphia: American Baptist Publication Society, 1907.

Walton, Robert C. *The Gathered Community.* London: Carey Press, 1946.

Wayland, Francis. *Principles and Practices of Baptist Churches.* New York: Sheldon, Blakeman and Company, 1857.

Weston, Henry G. *Constitution and Polity of the New*

Testament Church. Philadelphia: The American Bap-
tist Publication Society, 1895.
White, W. R. *Baptist Distinctives.* Nashville: The Sunday
School Board of the Southern Baptist Convention, 1946.
Wilkinson, William C. *The Baptist Principle in Application
to Baptism and the Lord's Supper.* Philadelphia: The
American Publication Society, 1897.

ARTICLES AND PERIODICALS

Minutes of the Philadelphia Baptist Association, ed. A.D.
Gillette (1851), pp. 25, 27, 77, 86.
Barnes, W. W. "American Baptist Ecclesiology," *Review
and Expositor,* Vol. 37 (April, 1940), pp. 133-140.
Carver, W. O. "The Baptist Conception of the Church,"
The Chronicle, Vol. 10 (January, 1947), pp. 1-4.
————. "A Church: The Church," *Review and Expositor,*
Vol. 48 (April, 1951), pp. 147-160.
Estep. William R. Jr. "A Baptist Reappraisal of Sixteenth
Century Anabaptists," *The Chronicle,* Vol. 6 (January,
1943), pp. 19-31.
Gates, John P. "The Association as It Affected Baptist Polity
in North America," *The Chronicle,* Vol. 6 (January,
1943), pp. 19-31.
Harkness, R. E. E. "Early Practices of the Baptists in Amer-
ica," *The Chronicle,* Vol. 7 (January, 1944), pp. 13-29.
Hopkins, C. Howard. "The Radical Heritage Among Bap-
tists." *Review and Expositor,* Vol. 53 (April, 1956), pp.
144-167.
Hudson, Winthrop. "The Associational Principle Among
Baptists," *Foundations.* Vol. 1 (January, 1958), pp. 10-23.
————. "Stumbling Into Disorder," *Foundations,* Vol. I
(April, 1958), pp. 45-71.
————. "The Ecumenical Spirit of Early Baptists," *Re-
view and Expositor,* Vol. 55 (April, 1958), pp. 182-195.
Maring, Norman. "Some Thoughts on Baptist Polity," *Re-
view and Expositor,* Vol. 52 (October, 1955), pp. 451-459.

Neuman, A. H. "History of the Baptist Organization," *Review and Expositor*, (July, 1911).

Price, Theron D. "The Church and the Churches." *Review and Expositor*, Vol. 52 (January, 1955), pp. 443-450.

Rowland, H. O. "Baptist Councils," *Baptist Quarterly Review*. Vol. 13 (October, 1891), pp. 669-677.

Torbet, Robert. "The Baptist Concept of the Church," *The Chronicle*, Vol. 15 (April, 1952), pp. 3-18.

————. "Baptist Thought About the Church." *Foundations*. Vol. I (April, 1958), pp. 18-37.

Wamble, Hugh. "The Beginning of Associational Life Among English Baptists," *Review and Expositor*, Vol. 54 (October, 1957), pp. 544-559.

————. "Inter-Relations of Seventeenth Century Baptists," *Review and Expositor*, Vol. 54 (July, 1957), pp. 407-425.

————. "Early English Baptist Sectarianism," *Review and Expositor*, Vol. 55 (January, 1958), pp. 59-69.

REPORTS

A Manual of the Northern Baptist Convention, 1908-1918, "Statement on Background of Proposed Reorganization of the American Baptist Convention, 1956," ed. W. C. Bitting (Philadelphia: American Baptist Publication Society).

Management Audit of the American Baptist Convention, N.Y., American Institute of Management, 1955.

Constitutional Convention Booklet, The American Baptist Churches of the Pacific Southwest, 1970.

Report of the Study Commission on Denominational Structure, American Baptist Convention, 1971.